Table of Co

WICCA
FOR BEGINNERS

A Guide To Safely Practice Rituals,
Magic & Witchcraft While Learning
About The True Wiccan History
and Beliefs

SERENA CROW

Wicca For Beginners

A Guide To Safely Practice Rituals, Magic & Witchcraft While Learning About The True Wiccan History and Beliefs

By Serena Crow

Introduction

Wicca is a nature-based religion that has its roots in ancient Pagan beliefs. The central focus of Wicca is Nature with all its elements, particularly the Moon, honouring of whose phases helps us stay grounded and in touch with our own cycles of life.

The concept of Mother Earth is particularly important for Wiccans and celebrating Sabbats, the 8 seasonal festivals, is a way of paying homage to the cycles of nature. At these times, Wiccans align themselves with the core life-giving energy of Nature.

There are many ways to practice Wicca. You can do it as part of a coven, or as a solitary witch. You can join groups which focus on particular rituals or you can choose a tradition whose core beliefs resonate most with your own.

However, regardless of the type of Wicca they practice, all Wiccans love and respect Nature and some form very personal relationships with animals (animal spirits), plants (spirit guides), or specific locations (the spirit of place) from which they draw energy, inspiration and guidance.

The highlight of the Wiccan year, and the most important of all their holidays is the Samhain, the Festival of the Dead. This Sabbat marks the beginning of the Wiccan New Year, as well as the time when the veil between the worlds of the dead and the living is thin, and it becomes easy to contact the dead.

Rituals are part of Wicca, and while you can do them as successfully in the privacy of your home, for special effect Wiccans go outdoors during the Moon phases which correspond with the spell they are casting. For example, during the New Moon they cast spells to boost new projects or relationships; during the Waning Moon they do spells to help them get rid of something or someone, eg debt or an unpleasant person, etc.

Besides living in harmony, the second most important goal of all Wiccans is to develop their intuition so they can easily pick up vibes from their environment and apply it when practicing magic. Unlike most religions which have strict rules how things should be done and how festivals should be marked, Wicca encourages their members to develop and nurture their intuition and use it to find the best way to commune with the world of spirit.

In this book you will find some basic guidelines how to cast spells, celebrate Sabbats and perform rituals, however, you should try and develop your own "inner wisdom" and become confident enough to start creating your own chants, rituals and spells, for they will be more effective than those someone else had created.

And finally, regardless of what many people believe, Wiccans practice White magic and their spells are not meant to cause harm. Most of the spells Wiccans cast are for personal protection or healing, or they use them to dispel negative energies from their environment.

Being a Wiccan is about learning how to tap into the cosmic energy, and channel it to where you want it to go.

Chapter 1 What is Wicca?

History of Wicca

Wicca is a religion based on rituals and beliefs practiced in Europe in pre-Christian times. In other words, Wicca is a reconstruction of how our ancestors celebrated divinity, marked special occasions, prayed for what they needed, and parted with their dead, before the monotheistic religions (eg Christianity, Judaism and Islam) became dominant form or religious expression.

There are still cultures who worship many gods (eg in Hinduism), who live according to the rhythms of nature (eg indigenous tribes of Siberia, and the Amazon), and whose religion sees sacred in all the nature and its elements (eg Taoism, Shinto, etc).

Although Wiccan rituals and beliefs vary with different traditions and paths, the focus of Wiccan spirituality is the fertility Goddess and her consort, a horned God. As fertility depends on natural elements, Wiccans honour the elements of nature – earth, air, fire, water, spirit – and their associated directions – North, East, South, West, Centre - when they cast a sacred Circle to hold a ritual.

Although witchcraft is part of Wicca, it doesn't mean that Wiccans are involved in Satanic rituals. Wiccans do not sacrifice animals, drink animal blood, or perform any kind of Black Magic. They celebrate life in all its forms, and do not believe in the devil, which is an element of Christian religion. The Wiccan religion is pre-Christian when the term "devil" did not even exist (it was introduced with Christianity).

Wicca insists on strict moral codes of its members, promotes peace and harmony, and since all Wiccans honour Mother Earth as supreme deity, they care for the environment. Wicca teaches that if we learn to tap into the cosmic energy which is all around us, we can channel it in the direction we want it to go.

Wiccan Rede is the main ethical law of the religion, and the central message is: "Do no harm". In other words, don't join Wicca just so that you could learn to do spells to get back at someone, or to steal someone's husband or a job. One thing you should always remind yourself of is that whatever energy you send out, eventually comes back to you – both positive and negative. So, the Wiccan motto is "it pays to be kind".

Wiccan rituals used in Sabbats include a combination of meditation, chanting, praying and invocations. Depending on how much time, energy and resources you want to put into them, they can also include music, drumming, dancing, singing, etc.

Although celebration of Sabbats and spellcasting are main Wiccan activities, spiritual development is also an important element of Wicca. The main goal of all Wiccans is to develop their intuition, so as to be able to easily pick-up both positive and negative vibes from their environment. Once they can do that, they can use their intuition for healing or for attracting something they want, or if need be, to protect themselves from negative energies.

Covens are organized Wicca associations which follow a certain path. While there are many benefits of belonging to one, you can be just as successful as a solitary Wiccan, although it may take you longer to learn about rituals and spell casting.

Paths and Traditions

There are many ways of practicing Wicca, so you should try to find one whose core beliefs and practices you feel comfortable with. While some traditions insist on ritual participants performing rituals naked, others may be very pragmatic and not insist on details when doing magic. If you decide to follow a certain path, or to join a coven, make sure you know what their core values and expectations are. Choose the tradition that feels right for you and that you feel most comfortable with.

There are many traditions of Wicca, and for a beginner this may be very confusing. Two main schools of thought from which all other traditions came about are Gardnerian and Alexandrian.

Gardnerian Wicca

This tradition was founded by Gerald Gardner who is known as the father of modern Wicca. This is a pretty formal tradition which requires initiation and works with a degree system. Most of the information shared amongst the members is considered secret, and is not to be shared with anyone outside the tradition.

Alexandrian Wicca

This tradition was founded by Alex Sanders and is very similar to the Gardnerian Wicca, but it places more emphasis on ceremonial magic during Sabbats and Esbats. It, too, insists on formal initiation of new members, and practices a degree system.

Many other traditions of Wicca were derived from these two:

– British Traditional Wicca (Gardnerian, Alexandrian, Central Valley, Algard, and Blue Star Wicca)

– Eclectic Wicca

– Celtic Wicca

– Saxon Wicca

– Dianic Wicca

– Faery Wicca

– Georgian Wicca

– Odyssean Wicca

– Wiccan Church (New Reformed Orthodox Order of the Golden Dawn; Church and School of Wicca; Circle Sanctuary; Covenant of the Goddess; Aquarian Tabernacle Church; Rowan Tree Church; Covenant of Unitarian Universalists Pagans; Coven of the Far Flung Net).

Solitary Wiccans

If you are new to Wicca, it's best to start by focusing on core Wiccan beliefs and learning as much as you can about Wicca before you join a coven.

You can learn from books, magazines, online Wicca magazines, etc. Follow discussions among Wiccans on Forums to better understand what Wicca is about, and to find out answers to some of the questions you might have.

Wicca doesn't have strict rules and formal requirements, so it's not hard being a solitary Wiccan. However, you will be at a slight disadvantage compared to those who belong to a coven, because you'll miss out on group rituals.

6 things to focus on when you become a Wiccan:

? Intuition

Learn to listen to your intuition, and to trust your instincts. Intuition is that inner voice that usually knows what's best for us, the trouble is we usually ignore it.

? Wiccan Rede

Always remember that the main Wiccan Law is to do no harm. Cast a spell to get a job, but not the job that someone else has. Cast a spell to be left alone, but not to destroy the person who's annoying you, etc. In other words, it's OK to desire something, but it's wrong to want it so much that you're prepared to destroy other people's lives to get it.

Accept responsibility for your words, and actions, as well as for the consequences of your spells. Having the power to change reality (yours and other peoples') is a huge responsibility. Don't abuse these powers.

? Altar

As a Wiccan, you must have an altar, no matter how small. You don't need to invest huge amounts of money into this. You can find almost everything you need for your altar in your home or garden, eg instead of crystals you can use stones, instead of chalice you can use a cup, instead of fancy candles you can use an ordinary white candle, etc.

? Spell casting

If you decide not to belong to a coven or follow a specific path, that's OK. But, if you are going solo, start small. Start with simple spells, until you learn how to cast a circle, perform magic, do visualization, etc.

Start practicing spell casting by buying candles of different colour to represent different energies that need to be invoked in a ritual (eg red for passion, yellow for energy, green for health, etc). Next, start collecting objects you will use to mark the four quarters of the Circle which will represent the four elements (air, water, fire, earth), for example:

Air: feathers, images or figurines of birds, incense, etc.
Fire: candles, red glassware, red or orange crystals, etc.
Water: bowl of water, blue items, seashells, image of fish, etc.
Earth: crystals, stones, brown or yellow items, leaves, etc.

? Sabbats

Start celebrating Sabbats. These are times of the year which mark the changing of the seasons. There are 8 Sabbats and you may choose to celebrate all of them, or just one or two. You can make elaborate preparations for Sabbats, or you can simply mark the occasion by lighting a candle (or a fire if you have a garden), leaving some offerings for Mother Earth (eg bird seed, or some food for stray or wild animals) and giving thanks.. By celebrating the seasons you are honoring Mother Earth.

? Divinity

Understand that the Divine is all around you. Everything is sacred. Everyone is sacred. Respect that. Don't ever do anything that could destroy or harm the environment and its creatures.

Witches and Witchcraft

The term "witch" comes from the Anglo-Saxon word "wicca" meaning "wise". Witches, therefore, are the "wise" women and witchcraft is the "craft of the wise". The reason witches were referred to as wise women, is that they usually possessed considerable knowledge of healing herbs and spells which could help people. In ancient times, witches were both healers and counsellors.

Although witchcraft is a widely misunderstood term, it usually refers to someone who possesses magical powers, who practices of sorcery, and who communes with spirits and deities.

The reason that formal religions (eg Christianity, Judaism and Islam) fought such a vengeful war on Pagans is that they believed that practicing witchcraft enabled people to influence other people's mind and body against their will. Their ability to cast spells were ridiculed but also feared, as was their ability to contact the spirits of the dead, and their involvement in divination and prophecy.

During the witch hunt of the Middle Ages, tens of thousands of these wise women were killed at the stake throughout the Western Europe where the Catholic Church felt threatened by this female power. It's mind boggling to think how much esoteric knowledge was lost this way.

Together with the wise women, hundreds of thousands of cats were killed as well, for they were believed to be part of witchcraft. Science has in the meantime found out that such massive destruction of cats in Western Europe during the Middle Ages, was probably the main reason the plague killed millions of people there. The bubonic plague was caused by infected fleas and lice which lived on rats, and with no cats to get rid of them, the plague spread like fire.

Sociologists also believe that one of the reason the Catholic church was consumed with such fanatical fear and hatred of Paganism, which resulted in hysterical witch hunt, was because in Pagan traditions, men and women are seen as equal. That was against the core beliefs of the Church which saw women as inferior in relation to men, and who therefore perceived these beliefs as a real threat to the Patriarchal system. Therefore, witch hunt was also the war against the power of women.

Wiccan Rede

Although Wicca doesn't have strict dogmas their members have to follow, they do live by certain rules.

Wiccan Laws of the craft:

? Witches practice rituals and rites primarily to attune themselves with the natural rhythm of life, and not to do magic which will alter the reality – theirs or other people's.

? Being able to align themselves with this rhythm of nature, gives witches a responsibility toward the environment. They seek to live in harmony with Nature and protect it. So, in a way, witches were our first environmental activists. This is in complete contrast to the anthropocentrism of the Biblical traditions that assumes human superiority over nature.

? Witches believe that supernatural power is within the reach of those who know and want to tap into it.

? Witches believe in harmony, and this includes the divinity. They believe that both genders have to be present during rituals, which is why they summon both the Goddess and her consort, the God. Sex is a normal part of life, always has been and always will be, so this is nothing to be ashamed of or feel guilty about.

? Witches recognize the existence of both the physical and spiritual world. Magic happens when you learn how to successfully interact between the two.

? Although some covens do have High Priestesses, generally speaking witches do not recognize any authoritarian hierarchy. However, they do honor those who teach and share their knowledge and wisdom.

? For witches, magic is part of life and witchcraft is the Wiccan way.

? You cannot inherit the position of a witch from a family member, you have to become a witch in your own right. However, just by calling yourself a witch does not make you one. You become one through knowledge and skill of witchcraft.

? Witches do not recognize the concept of absolute evil, entities known as Satan or the Devil are part of Christian dogma. However, witches believe in negative forces and energies which they dispel with the help of banishing ritual magic.

? Witches honor Nature and believe that everything we need for our health and wellbeing can be found there.

? The Goddess manifests in three forms as a Maiden, Mother, and Crone.

? Each Goddess has a consort, or as some call him, a husband.

? That as long as you harm no one, you can do what you like. This is the law.

? Witches are bound by the Threefold Law: whatever you create, be it laughter or pain, joy or sorrow, is returned to you threefold.

? Witches seek to live in harmony, not only with each other, but with the Earth, that which is our womb and our home.

? That death is NOT the end of existence, but a step in the ongoing circle of life.

? That there is NO sacrifice of blood, for she is the mother of All living things and from all things proceed unto her, and unto her, all things return. Killing is for survival and defense only.

? Wiccans do not seek converts. The Way is open to those, who, for whatever reason, seek and find the craft.

Wiccan Tools

Wiccan tools are essential for magic rituals, but not in the way that is usually believed. The tools of trade can range from a single piece of crystal, to an altar full of various symbols, special clothes, headdress, and jewelry.

Although you will need certain tools to perform a ritual, what's much more important for the spell to work is the power of your intent. In themselves, tools do not possess magic, but they do possess the power to change your subconscious, and create a certain atmosphere in which you can relax enough and focus sufficiently to achieve the desired outcome.

Therefore, the best way to regard tools is like a medium which can help you relax, concentrate, or "switch off", so you can open your mind and heart to the world of spirit. For this reason, tools are a very personal thing and regardless of how simple (eg feather, unusual pieces of wood, a beautiful stone you picked up on a beach), or fancy (eg scented or colour candles, rare crystals, expensive athame or sword, etc) they are, they are your "door" to the world of spirit. Therefore, treat them with respect.

How to look after your ritual tools:

> ? Keep them clean

> ? Charge them occasionally

> ? Keep them away from sunlight when not using them

> ? Don't let others touch them

? Keep them wrapped in a cloth, or individually in case of crystals, when not using them

So, which tools to keep on your altar? This depends on what you hope to achieve, and how much money you are prepared to put into your tools collection.

The basic Wiccan tools of trade are:

? **Altar**

Ideally, altars should be kept in a room used only for rituals, but very few people can afford that. Instead, choose a corner of a room you spend most time in. You can place it on a table, coffee table, window sill, mantle piece, on the floor, even inside a drawer. Choose a place where you'll be able to easily reach the displayed objects, and where they will not be seen or touched by others.

You can set up a permanent altar, or create one only when you want to cast a spell or celebrate Sabbat.

A permanent altar is usually placed somewhere where you will often see it, and it should contain items which symbolise the four elements, plus anything else you feel should be there.

When setting up altar for a special occasion, you will use items characteristic of that particular intent. For example, if casting a love spell, you can represent the earth element with rose quartz crystal, the fire element with a red candle, etc.

For a job spell you may represent the earth element with a green crystal, such as malachite, fire element with a green candle, etc. For good luck spells focus on orange colour, for money spells focus on earth element and symbolic colours of brown, dark yellow, etc.

The most common items to be kept on an altar are:

? A chalice (or a goblet, cup, glass or a small bowl) to hold a drink

? A pentacle (or a picture or a drawing of a five-pointed star)

? A cauldron (or a small ceramic bowl) for mixing herbs and/or essences

? A small bell or a rattle

? Images or a symbolic representation of Goddess and God (eg statue, candles or whatever you decide should represent deities of your choice on your altar)

? Candles (or small lamp)

The items displayed on the altar can range from very expensive ones you get from specialised shops, or from items you find in your home or garden. It's important that all the items you decide to use have a special meaning to YOU, and it doesn't really matter how sophisticated or simple they are. Altar is a sacred place, in front of which you will pray, chant, contact the dead or enter into altered state of consciousness, so it should consist of ritual tools which you can use to this effect.

The purpose of altar items:

? Athame

This ceremonial blade usually has a black handle and represents the main ritual tool used in Wicca. Its main purpose is to channel and direct psychic energy during Wiccan rituals.

Athame is traditionally used for casting a circle, and should never be used for cutting. Whenever you want to buy something for Wiccan rituals (a knife, crystal, wand, etc) hold it in your hand for a few moments before buying it. Make sure it sends no negative energy. But, even if you feel fine while holding it, as soon as you get home cleanse and consecrate it.

? Pentacle

This is a flat disk in the shape of the five-pointed star, usually made of metal or wood. It is used as a symbol of protection or as a tool to evoke spirits. Some Wiccans hang it over doors and windows for additional protection.

? Candles

Candle color should match the energy you are trying to invoke (eg red for passion, blue for calm, green for health, etc), although white ones can always be used as a substitute.

Candles represent the Fire and Air elements and are essential for all rituals. It's best to use candles made of natural wax, and for basic spells you will need a collection of white, black, green, red, yellow, blue, gold and silver candles.

? Crystals

These are an important part of many rituals but as they are good conductors or energy, make sure you regularly cleanse and charge them. This is particularly important for stones used in spellwork. Don't let others touch them. If they do (people often want to hold beautiful things and examine them from up close), cleanse and recharge them as soon as you can.

? The Wand

This is used for casting a circle. If you don't have one, you can use the athame, or even your own hand, with pointed forefinger. It's usually made of wood because wood is an excellent conductor of energy and magic.

? Bells

Many Wiccans use bells in their rituals, because with bells they can create or raise vibrations, something you need a lot of for a successful ritual.

? Drums & rattles

You can cleanse someone's aura or free a space of negative energy by shaking a rattle and asking the Goddess to help you with cleansing. The vibrations created by drumming or by shaking rattles can dislodge negative energy that may have collected in the area where the spell is to be cast. Drums and rattles are often used in house-cleaning ceremonies, to free them of the previous occupants' energies.

? Herbs & oil

Some rituals call for herbs to be burned during a spell. Essential oils are used for anointing candles, the altar or the body in spell working.

By letting others touch your ritual tools, you are risking having traces of other people's aura or negative energy be transferred to you tools, intentionally or not. If you feel that might have happened, cleanse and recharge your tools before using them.

For this reason it's best to keep your altar somewhere where others won't see it and ask to hold what's on it. Treat your Wiccan tools with respect. Charge them to align them with your own aura, so they are happy to "work" for you when you next need to channel energy during a ritual.

Chapter 2 The Five Sacred Elements

Symbolism in Wicca

The four elements through which the world is seen in Wicca, represent the four qualities that are present in all of us, as well as in the world around us. These elements can be viewed physically or metaphysically.

The four elements are:

? Air

? Water

? Earth

? Fire

There is also the fifth element Spirit, or Aether, which, unlike the Air, Fire, Water and Earth is intangible, although present in all things. Spirit is the binding force that connects all other elements, and symbolically, it represents a "union".

From the physical point of view, elements are what we are surrounded with. Each of them is essential for our survival. We need air to breath, water represents 70% of our body mass, earth is what we walk on and grow our crops on, and fire keeps us warm and helps us prepare our meals. And the spirit makes the life worth living.

From the metaphysical point of view, these elements make who we are. Fire adds warmth and passion to our character, air helps us be intellectual and communicate successfully (both verbally and non-verbally), earth makes us "down to earth" and keeps us grounded, and water element boosts our creativity and imagination. And the spirit gives us joy.

What has all this got to do with Wicca?

Spellcasting is an important element of a Wiccan belief system and represents our attempt to change the physical reality according to our will. To this effect, we use a combination of intention and channelling.

The power of intention is key for successful spell casting, and the more powerful the intention, the more successful the spell. Concentration is key, and experienced Wiccan practitioners learn how to maintain their full concentration throughout the ritual even if it lasts for hours.

4 things that affect your concentration:

? Focus

Focus is very important, and to be focused you have to know what you want. This is more difficult than you may realize, for our desires are often not clear to us, so how can you expect the universe to hear you and help you achieve what you want if you can't put it down in words. To check how focused you are, think of something you would like to cast a spell for. Then, write down your intention in one line. Write down exactly what you want, and be as specific as you can. For example, instead of "I want a job", say "I want a job in *General Motors*, with a salary of $5,000 per month". Or, instead of "I'd like to have a new love", try describing the person you'd like to meet: their character, age, hobbies, even physical looks. Before asking the Universe to help you, make sure you know what you are looking for, because vague requests, give vague results.

? Patience

This is the most difficult part. With spells you have to be prepared to wait. Some wishes can be granted within a day or two, for others you may have to wait for months. What should you do while you wait? Some believe that it's enough to cast a spell and wait for it to be manifested, but most Wiccans recommend "reminding" the Universe about your spell. Rather than just casting a spell and then waiting for the result, repeat the spell at regular intervals until you get what you asked for. When you repeat the spell, don't keep on changing what you are asking for, but stick to the original request.

? Realism

When you want something, always bear in mind that you have to be realistic. Simply wishing for something is not enough. You won't get a job by repeatedly casting job spells. You have to look for a job, make sure you have the skills, knowledge and experience required for that job, and then cast spells to boost your confidence and increase your chances of doing well in the interview. You won't find new love by staying at home and dreaming about it. You have to go out, meet people, and not neglect your physical appearance. This doesn't mean you shouldn't dream big, but be realistic and don't expect miracles overnight. As someone once said, "You have to help luck find you".

? Channelling

The energy (mental, emotional and spiritual) you put in a spell, needs to be channelled so it goes where you want it to go. Before casting a spell, consider what you want to achieve with it, which tools you will need, do you need to prepare certain mantras, which deities you are going to ask for help, etc. Go through the ritual in your head before you get down to it, because once you cast a Circle and invoke the elements, there won't be time to think about the practicalities, nor should you change what you are casting the spell for half way through the ritual. Make sure you are mentally and emotionally prepared for the ceremony.

Spell casting can be an energy-consuming activity, especially for a novice, for it involves different procedures (chanting, mantras, invocations, etc) and sometimes lasts for hours. The reason we invoke elements in a ritual is to help us stay focused on what we are doing. For example, if you are dealing with love issues, focusing on the element of fire will help you direct and channel your energy where you want it to go.

However, magic doesn't happen only during spell casting. By simply keeping symbols of certain elements near you (eg carrying a piece amethyst in your pocket to help you deal with stress, wearing a rose quartz pendant when searching for love, using herbs or essential oils to help you relax or have prophetic dreams, etc), you are keeping yourself aligned with your intent even when you are not casting a spell.

Symbols of each of the elements can be kept on your altar all the time, or you can display them only during a spell casting ritual. Alternatively, you may choose to wear or carry symbols of elements on your person, or keep them in your desk, car or a bag.

The Element of Air

Symbolically, air represents intellect and creativity and is traditionally symbolized by feathers, incense, bells, wind chimes, bird figurines or images, and anything else that to you represents this element.

Ideally, these items should be in the colour symbolic of the element of Air, such as grey, white, blue and light yellow. If you have nothing to represent this element with, you can simply use the colour to represent this element (eg a piece of blue cloth, a sheet of white paper, etc).

Air is used to cleanse and clear, both physically and metaphysically. Physically we need fresh air to clear the stagnant air in a room, but we also say "His arrival was like a breath of fresh air", or "We need to clear the air between us before we start discussing new plans".

Metaphysically, the element of air is used as a symbol of purification and transformation. However, nature requires moderation in everything. Too much air creates chaos and destruction (eg strong wind or draft). So, in spellwork, just like in life, you need to maintain balance.

In ritual, you can focus on the element of Air when you are doing spells concerning study, interviews, legal matters, children, communication, and travel. You can also focus on this element when casting spells to mark new birth, new relationship, or to invite something into your life.

The Element of Water

The element of Water is often used to represent emotions and inner harmony. The importance of water in our life is evident from the fact that about 70% of our body mass is water, and that over 70%of the earth is covered in water. While water means life, too much of it creates chaos (eg flooding, violent storms, tsunamis, etc).

In spellwork we invoke the element of Water to bring balance to our emotions and the colours we use to represent this element are blue, white, and pale grey.

In ritual, water stands for intuition and inner wisdom, so this element needs to be invoked every time you cast spells to heal emotions, boost your creativity or do soul search.

The best symbols of water to use on your altar or in spells is the water itself (eg a glass of water), or just an empty water container (eg a glass or a cup).

The Element of Earth

Earth is solid and grounding and is traditionally represented by a piece of rock, a crystal, a handful of earth, a piece of wood, leaves, cones, pebbles, flowers, herbs, etc.

The element of Earth is invoked when casting spells to bring stability and security to your family or business. Earth element is used for all money-relating issues, but can also be used in healing spells which require grounding, eg after a trauma or a particularly stressful situation.

When doing spells for issues concerning earth-related matters, you need to focus on the symbolic items representing this element. However, if you have long-standing earth-related problems (eg you are constantly short of money, or you move from one relationship to another), place earth symbols all over your home to balance and stabilize your life.

The Element of Fire

In ritual, fire stands for strength and passion, but also for aggression and destruction. Symbols of fire are candles, athame and some crystals, and colours used to represent this element are red, orange, yellow and gold.

Symbolically, fire represents action and energy, but should be used with caution, for too much fire brings destruction. It's often used as a symbol of passionate love (traditionally red roses and rose quartz are used for love spells), but also for strength and fury (eg we say "to see red" when describing someone who's very angry).

However, fire works both ways. Although it symbolize aggression and anger, it is also used in spells to banish anger. By focusing on the destructive aspect of fire, we can successfully get rid of destructive things, emotions or situations (eg pain, debt, toxic relationship).

So, perhaps more than with other elements, we need to carefully balance the amount of fire in our lives, as well as in our spells. While a little bit of fire in life makes it more exciting and interesting, too much of it creates choleric temperament, and aggressive behaviour.

The Element of Spirit

Although invisible, the element of spirit is present in almost everything, and serves to connect us to the other four elements. You will need to focus on this element if casting spells to gain enlightenment, to find your life path, or discover hidden meaning of life.

Spirit is essential for our well-being and it represents something without which it is possible to live, but without which it is impossible to feel fulfilled.

Colours to use when invoking this element are purple or white. Symbolically, you can represent this element with a pentacle, cord, infinity sign, or the wheel. In the positive sense, spirit boosts your wisdom, intuition and sixth sense, but the negative aspect of this element is that it can lead to self-destructive behaviours.

In spellwork, this element should be used sparingly, and only to help you balance your energy but never for magical purposes.

The Elementals

Each of the five elements has its own elemental. Elementals are nature spirits which exist on a different astral plane, and their roles in life, or spells, vary. We usually invoke them during spell work if we feel we need additional support to achieve something. While Goddess is invoked in all spells, elementals are brought in when dealing with more difficult issues.

Elementals can be found everywhere where there is greenery, but are particularly prominent in peaceful, unpolluted and isolated locations.

In ancient times, there was a universal belief in spirits which inhabit Nature, and for many indigenous cultures whose religion is based on animism, they are still very real. These spirits can attach themselves to everything, but are invisible to humans, except for those with psychic abilities.

Simply put, elementals are non physical entities which exist in the mental or astral plane. They are very much part of our life, although we now refer to them as "thought forms".

We know that thoughts produce vibrations, and these are reflected in our aura. Clairvoyants and intuitives can "read" auras and see, or simply intuitively sense, what kind of elementals (ie thought-forms) a person lives with.

When can you invoke elementals in ritual?

? When you are clear what you need help with (eg do you need strength, wisdom, or stability)

? When you know which elementals support which elements, so you know who to ask for help (eg fairies for the Air element, gnomes for the Earth element, etc)

? When you understand which element and elementals correspond to the aspect of your life you need help with (eg Fire elementals, such as dragons and salamanders, can be summoned to add strength and energy)

4 types of elementals:
  ? **Earth elementals**

Dwarves, giants, trolls, gnomes or goblins are elementals living in the soil, beneath tree roots and in rocks. They stabilize and heal the land, bringing stability and calm. You will need their help in situations or spells which require grounding, strength and firmness.

? **Air elementals**

These are sylphs and fairies and can be found on mountain tops, in trees and flowers. We invoke them for spells dealing with communication, insight and mental clarity.

? **Fire elementals**

The best known ones are dragons, phoenixes and salamanders. They purge and cleanse with fire, so work with them in moderation.

? **Water elementals**

These are mermaids, sirens and udines. They are found in rivers, seas, fountains, and help regulate flow of water. You can ask for their help with spells dealing with emotions or inner work.

In magic, elementals are symbols of purity and are visible only to those who exist on the same frequency (ie clairvoyants and intuitives). However, some elementals are believed not to be very friendly to people, and to enjoy causing accidents and problems.

They easily attach themselves to almost anything, or anyone, so some witches use them as psychic vampires and send them to attach themselves on other people's auras, causing them misfortune and draining them of energy.

Be careful when working with these entities, for just like with other aspects of magic, you have to know what you're getting yourself into, especially if you want to use magic to hurt or punish someone.

Although very few people believe in them, elementals are very real, only now we call them "thought forms" or "energies".

Chapter 3 Deities

Nature Worship

Many refer to Wicca as a nature religion, however, although Wiccans have great respect for nature and all its elements (eg mountains, rivers, trees, the Sun, the Moon, etc), they don't worship Nature. However, there is a lot of similarity between nature worship and Wicca.

As a religion, nature worship is based on the veneration of natural phenomena, eg the Sun, the Moon, the stars, wind, rivers, fire, etc. During pre-Christian times, this was the way our ancestors communicated with the Higher Power.

Even today, many cultures still worship various aspects of Nature:

? Zoroastrians worship fire (ie the Sun),

? Shinto religion of Japan revolves around the worship of nature and nature spirits,

? The Taoists worship all natural phenomena,

? The Hindu worship many Gods as well as life-giving water (river Ganga),

? Spirituality of the indigenous tribes of Siberia and the Amazon focuses on animism

? The Australian Aborigines' spirituality emphasizes the importance of landscape (spirit of place)

This shows that despite all the persecution, nature religions are still going strong. Unfortunately, original Pagan rituals are not well documented, but we can learn about them by studying the indigenous cultures that still exist today.

The interesting thing is that for most of indigenous peoples the concept of "nature" does not exist. They simply see everything around them, what we refer to as "nature", as part of their world, eg mountains, lakes, rocks, forests, animals, etc. They do not make distinction between nature and culture, for them it is all one.

In their world, spots which are for some reason unusual and stand out from the rest of the landscape (eg unusual rock formation, a particularly deep cave, an ancient tree, etc), are believed to be inhabited by sacred spirits. Over time, these phenomena become objects of worship, eg mountain tops, trees, waterfalls and locations where they are found become shrines under the sky.

According to Earth-based cultures, Nature is the most sacred thing in the world. It is permeated with spirits, and in order to be in contact with these spirits, one should be in contact with nature.

Early people were very attached to their landscapes, mainly because they believed that everything around them had a soul, so they lived sustainibly and looked after their environment. We now realize that as guardians of ancient forests, rivers and mountains, early people were the first environmental activists.

Duality of Worship: Gods and Goddesses

Some Wiccans worship only the Goddess, however, most believe that both the feminine and the masculine aspects of divinity should be invoked in ritual (eg in Hinduism, every Goddess has a consort, and the same was true in all pre-Christianity religions).

Honouring both the Goddess and the God is part of the balance in nature. Besides, we all possess both masculine and feminine qualities, so by honouring deities of both gender you are honouring both sides of yourself.

However, for women it is usually easier to focus on the Goddess in their rituals, and for man the focus on the God, and that is fine, as long as you don't ignore the other gender completely.

Summoning the Goddess and the God is one of the first things you do, after you cast a Circle and mark the four quarters. The deities need to be present as witnesses of your ritual, and as a sign that you have created a sacred space.

Wicca religion focuses on the Goddess and that's how our ancestors who lived 35,000 years ago (and earlier) honoured life. We know this from a number of archaeological artefacts, in the form of female figurines or drawings, which were found throughout Europe. This proves that until about 3000 years ago (which means for most of the time man has existed on earth), people worshipped Mother Goddess, or Mother Earth.

It was only with the arrival of patriarchal, warlike Indo European tribes, who migrated from the area around the Caspian Sea, and spread throughout Europe and Asia, that the focus of worship shifted from female to male deities.

As mentioned earlier, Wicca is a religion recreated on the basis of historical and archaeological evidence of paganism in Europe, so most of the Goddesses and Gods worshipped by Wiccans stem from the ancient Celtic, Egyptian, Mesopotamian, or ancient Greek and Roman female deities.

However, Wiccans also often choose to honour deities from other religions, eg Hinduism, Buddhism, Taoism, etc.

Since religion is a very personal experience, when deciding who to worship, choose a deity you feel most comfortable with, the one you can relate to. However, many indigenous people dislike the fact that Christians are starting to worship their deities, and copy, often poorly, the ancient ceremonies. They find this offensive and suggest that everyone should worship Pagan deities of their own ancestry. So, if you're a German, you should focus on ancient Norse Goddesses and Gods. Italians should worship the deities of ancient Rome, the French the ancient Celtic deities, etc.

However, for a number of reasons we sometimes feel closer to deities of other cultures than to those from the culture we originally come from. But, the most important thing when choosing a Goddess and God to invoke in your rituals, is that you feel drawn to that particular deity. It's easy to find all the information about individual deities on Internet, so the list below is just a brief guide to female deities.

However, since everything around us changes all the time, so do we and our circumstances, so don't feel bad if after a while you decide to change the focus of your worship. Alternatively, you may choose to invoke deities from different cultures for different occasions.

For example, for luck you can invoke Fortuna, for love spells ask Ishtar to help, when you need strength to overcome a major hurdle ask for Rhiannon, for healing spells invoke Brighid, for peace at home pray to Hestia, for marriage troubles contact Hera, to pass an exam call upon Saraswati, for wealth spells summon Lakshmi, etc.

However, it is best if you choose one female and one male deity, who will represent your Matron and Patron deities, and whom you will invoke in all (or most) your rituals.

6 cultures that the best known female deities come from:

1. Celtic culture

2. Ancient Egypt

3. Ancient Near East (Mesopotamia)

4. Ancient Greek

5. Ancient Roman

6. Hindu

The most important Goddesses and the areas of life they can help with:

Celtic Goddesses

- Brighid - a goddess of fertility, healing and crafts

- Rhiannon – a goddess of the hunt, horses, strength, and the moon

- Danu — Irish Mother Goddess

- Cerridwen — Celtic Goddess of transformation, inspiration, and prophecy

- Rosmurta — Celtic Goddess of abundance and business success

Egyptian Goddesses

- Isis - Egyptian Mother Goddess, mother of all nature, magic and children

- Ma'at – Egyptian Goddess of justice, order and balance

- Hathor — Egyptian Goddess of childbirth and death

Mesopotamian Goddesses

- Astarte — Phoenician Goddess of fertility, sexuality, and war

- Inanna/Ishtar — Sumerian Goddess of passionate love, fertility, and war

Ancient Greece Goddesses

- Hecate – Greek Goddess of witchcraft, magic and the Moon

- Athena — Greek Goddess of wisdom, and war

- Selene — Greek Goddess of the Moon

- Sophia — Greek Goddess of wisdom

- Gaia — The Greek Mother Goddess

- Hestia — Greek Goddess of the home and domestic life

- Aphrodite — Greek Goddess of love and beauty

Ancient Rome Goddesses

- Diana - Roman Goddess of the Moon and the hunt, childbirth, but also a fierce warrior, she represents the strong feminine aspect of life

- Venus – Roman Goddess of love and beauty

- Fortuna — Roman Goddess of fortune

- Luna — Roman Goddess of the Moon

- Hera — Roman Goddess of the hearth, marriage, and women

- Minerva — Roman Goddess of wisdom and war

- Voluptas — Roman Goddess of pleasure

Hindu Goddesses

- Annapurna — Hindu Goddess of nourishment, can help nourish your body as well as the soul

- Durga — Hindu Great Goddess, Divine Mother

- Kali — Hindu Goddess of time and death, slayer of demons, destroys and protects

- Lakshmi — Hindu Goddess of wealth and prosperity

- Lalita — Hindu Goddess of beauty

- Saraswati — Hindu Goddess of knowledge, the arts, education, and wisdom

- Shakti — Hindu primordial cosmic energy, Great Divine Mother

Wiccan Goddesses often have titles, such as:

? Crone Goddess

These deities watch over eternal Wisdom, eg life, death, and rebirth (eg Cerridwen, Hecate)

? Earth Goddess

These deities represent the Earth itself, eg Gaia, Cybele, etc.

? Great Mother Goddess/Divine Mother

These are usually the chief female deities in most Pagan religions, eg Gaia, Isis, Parvati, etc.

Animism

To better understand Wicca, you have to understand the concept of animism.

Animism is the belief that everything around us has life force or energy, eg rocks, trees, streams, animals, heavenly bodies, etc.

According to this spiritual approach everything around us has a soul or spirit, and these spirits, that make these things alive, need to be worshipped, or placated by offerings so they would continue to give favours, offer protection, or help people.

There are still cultures which practice animism, eg Shinto, Hinduism, Taoism, and indigenous religions of Siberia, Africa and South America.

While they lived as hunter-gatherers, people were entirely dependant on nature and regarded themselves as part of it. So, everything that existed in nature, eg rivers, animals, mountains, they regarded as beings not very different from themselves. For this reason, early man related to all living and nonliving things as his equal, and this is why he treated nature and its elements with respect and reverence.

Hunters depend on animals for their survival, so early men regularly performed rituals to give thanks to the source of food without which they could not exist. They honoured the animals they hunted, as well as the rain which helped the grass grow, which the animals they hunted needed to feed on.

When people settled down and started practicing agriculture, they tried to win the favour of the spirits that provided rain so their crops would grow, and their livestock multiply. For early man, everything in Nature was related and connected, and they themselves were an integral part of this web of life.

Most animistic cultures believe that spirit survives physical death and continues to live, usually in a place where it's always warm, where there is plenty of food, etc. On the other hand the spirits who for some reasons refused, or were prevented from leaving the earth, remain in their communities as malignant spirits, ie ghosts, who haunt the living and cause accidents and bad luck. For this reason, great effort is put into ensuring the dead are buried in a way that would guarantee they leave the earth for good.

Followers of animism believe that the soul may return to avenge its death or to seek vengeance for itself. So, if a place becomes haunted, it is usually by a ghost of someone who had died a violent death, and had become a malignant spirit.

Highly animistic religions have sophisticated rituals to repel these spirits from causing harm to the living. Ancestor worship present in many formal religions of today, is a subtle way of placating the spirits of the dead so they would help, rather than cause harm to their communities.

Chapter 4 Wheel of the Year

Wiccan Holidays - Days of Power

For those living close to nature, or as part of nature, the change of seasons is an important moment in their calendar year. When the amount of light available during the day starts dwindling, it's a signal to animals, plants as well as people, that season is about to change.

The power of Sun played a major role in life of early man. Long before the first civilizations started springing up along the Tigris and Euphrates or the Nile, man worshipped the life-giving Sun. That animistic worship later changed into early religions where sun- or fire-worship was the dominant aspect of religion (eg in Egypt and in Zoroastrianism).

For early man, and for modern Wiccans, life revolves around certain times of the year, when the seasons change. There were a number of seasonal festivals celebrated at, or around the solstice and equinox dates.

Veneration of the Sun takes many forms, and is still widely celebrated throughout the world, although often in disguise. Many of the festivals of the dominant religions are nothing more than disguised ancient Pagan celebrations of arrival of spring (Easter), winter (Christmas), Samhain (All Souls Day), etc.

The festivals celebrated on or around the solstice and equinox dates make up the Wheel of the Year, and are called Sabbats.

From the scientific point of view, there is a reason why these times were so important not just for early man, but until about 100 years ago, for all agriculturalists. Simply put, the Wheel of the Year is nothing more than a division of active and dormant parts of the year.

Our ancestors had a close relationship with Nature, partly because they had to (they depended on Her for survival), and partly because they saw themselves as part of Nature and did not make too much distinction between themselves (as humans) and other living organisms (eg animals, plants, lakes, etc).

When you live close to Nature (whether because you want to, or have to), you need to adapt your lifestyle and activities to Her cycles. This is why the earliest festivals celebrated the rhythms of nature, and marked the close relationship between man and his environment.

So what happens during a Sabbat celebration? Like so much in Wicca, the details can vary widely, but generally speaking, there is a ritual focusing on some element of the God/Goddess relationship, and the season. For example, Spring and Summer Sabbats focus on themes of fertility and abundance, while Autumnal Sabbats are related to harvesting and weakening of the Sun.

The formal Sabbat ritual is usually followed by a feast and merrymaking. The ritual itself may be simple or elaborate, and may involve just a few practitioners, or hundreds of people.

Solitary Wiccans are at a disadvantage because they have to make all the preparations and perform all the rituals themselves. On the other hand, they are free to choose which Sabbat to celebrate and how much energy and money to put into the celebrations. Many decide to mark each Sabbat by a simple thanksgiving ritual, for after all, the purpose of Sabbats is to honour the Goddess, and align yourself to the forces of Nature.

By celebrating Sabbats, and there is one every six weeks, you are unconsciously becoming more attuned to Nature, as you are forced to observe the change of seasons more closely.

However, today, when food is readily available, and we live in brightly-lit and warm apartments, we don't relate to the harvest or the arrival of spring the same way our ancestors did. Seasonal changes have lost their importance, especially for city dwellers, still, Sabbats also carry symbolic meaning and we can use these times to align our spell casting to the seasons.

For example, Winter solstice is a good time for innerwork, while Summer solstice is a powerful time for health, wealth and abundance spells. During Spring equinox (when there is equilibrium between the length of the day and night) we can cast spells for inner balance, and during Lammas (harvest time) we contemplate and give thanks for everything we've achieved so far.

Sabbats

We know there were 8 of these ancient festivals, or Sabbats, although not all cultures celebrated all of them, nor were they celebrated at the same time, or in the same manner.

Today, Wiccans observe these 8 Sabbats as two groups of festivals:

– The Fire Festivals (or cross quarter festivals)

These include Imbolc, Beltane, Lammas and Samhain. Cross quarter days fall half way between an equinox and solstice.

– The Solar Festivals (or quarter festivals)

These are two solstices (Litha and Yule), and two equinoxes (Ostara and Mabon).

The four Fire Festivals:

1) **Imbolc**

Imbolc was celebrated on 1 and 2 February, but Christians turned this celebration into St Brighid's Day or Candlemas. In February days start getting longer, so this festival marks the end of winter and the beginning of spring. The Imbolc celebrations focus on the strengthening of the Sun.

2) Beltane

Beltane marked the beginning of Summer. It took place in early May and is now replaced by the 1 May holiday. This is the time of spring rains and greening of the earth, and Beltane celebrations focus on the fertility of Nature.

On this day, all around us we witness the union of the God and the Goddess and the new life that the sacred marriage produces. Traditionally, this union is symbolized by the dance around the Maypole.

3) Lughnasadh/Lammas

This festival marked the time of first harvest and took place on 1 and 2 August. This was a time of major thanksgiving celebrations. There are still many local festivals celebrated at this time. Traditionally, people prayed and offered sacrifice for the success of future crops, and symbolically what you've achieved by Lammas is your main achievement for the year.

4) Samhain

This festival was known as the witches' New Year, the Pagan new year starts from Samhain. Symbolically, this is a time when you have a chance to begin anew.

Samhain is also the time to remember the dead. This is believed to be a magical time when the veil between the world of the dead and the living is thin and when contacting the dead is easy. In rituals performed at this time one must honor, remember and speak of the dead. Christianity replaced Samhain with All Soul's Day festival.

Spiritually, winter is a time for turning inwards, ie for reflecting both on the summer behind us, and the spring ahead of us.

The Four Solar Festivals

1. Winter Solstice (Yule) - 20/21 December

This marks the shortest day of the year. The focus of this Sabbat is the return of the Sun, and from winter solstice days become longer by approximately 2 minutes each day.

In terms of spellwork, winter is considered a good time for grounding and inner work, as well as for banishing spells.

2. Spring Equinox (Ostara) – 21/22 March

On this day, Wiccans celebrate the arrival of Spring and the earth's awakening from a long, harsh winter. The focus of this Sabbat is rebirth.

This marks the time when hours of light and darkness are equal, so symbolically, spring equinox is a good time to seek equilibrium within. You can do spells for inner balance at this time.

3. Summer Solstice (Litha) – 21/22 June

This festival marks the longest day of the year and is also known as Midsummer.

From this day, days start becoming shorter (although the summer has just arrived), so we try to draw on the powerful, life-giving energy of the Sun.

In terms of spellwork, Summer solstice is a powerful time for all spells: health, wealth, love, and abundance. Rituals performed at this time mimic the power of the Sun.

The focus in Litha celebrations is on fire (representing the Sun), passion and abundance of life.

4. Autumn Equinox (Mabon) – 21/22 September

This is another time of the year when hours of light and darkness are equal.

This was the festival of the second harvest and during Mabon we give thanks for the days of plenty and warmth.

Symbolically, Mabon is the time of giving thanks for everything you have: health, family, friends, regular income, etc.

Some traditions of Wicca celebrate only Fire festivals, while others observe only the Solar festivals. Celebrating all eight Sabbats can be impractical, so choose the ones you feel most drawn to.

Esbats

There are also the Esbats, festivals which were celebrated on the 13 full moons that occur every year. These festivals celebrated the Goddess at her height of power, as Pagans believed that the Full Moon was the time when the Goddess magic was stronger than at any other day of the month.

The Moon is no less important than the Sun, and in witchcraft it's actually the other way round, with the Moon being the chief deity.

There is something about the Full Moon that cannot be explained in words. It's almost as if it has magic of its own, which is probably why people have worshipped under the Full Moon since time immemorial.

Actually, there is archaeological evidence that people have celebrated the Midwinter (Yule) for about 12,000 years, while the evidence of lunar calendars dates back to nearly 40,000 years. This ancient fascination with the Full Moon still lives in us, for the Full Moon somehow stimulates our primitive, atavistic urge to go out and stare at it, speechless.

Traditionally, Wicca covens meet on the Full Moon or the New Moon days. Solitary practitioners can celebrate both, or just one.

Early man was very observant of his environment and recognized the three phases of the Moon (Waxing, Full and Waning Moon), as a cycle of birth, death and renewal.

Each of the phases symbolizes one aspect of womanhood:

? The Waxing phase (when the moon is growing) represents the youthful aspect of the Goddess. Symbolically this phase relates to a strong, independent young woman who knows what she wants in life, and how to get it. This phase is about birth and growth.

? The Full Moon symbolizes the fullness of the mother aspect. This phase is about fertility, nourishment and protection of life.

? The Waning Moon represents the aged and wise crone aspect, a symbol of maturity, wisdom, intuition and healing.

As Wiccans celebrate different cycles of life, they also honor the three cycles of the Moon and draw on each one when doing magic. Different phases of the moon have different energy and symbolism, and Wiccans align with these phases in order to make the most of these specific energies and empower their spells:

– New Moon

The energy of this phase is used for personal growth, healing and blessing. Use this time for constructive magic, to begin something, create something new, or bless a new arrival (of a baby, a car, new home, etc)

– Waxing Moon

The energy of this phase is good for attracting something: magic, love, health, protection. Spells to do with growth (eg of business, love, education) are best cast at this time.

– Full Moon

This is a very powerful time to draw on the energy of the Moon to deal with major problems, decisions or personal crisis. Reserve the days of the Full Moon for spells that are really important for you, when you know you will need a major boost for anything you do. Don't waste the Full Moon days energy on minor issues.

– Waning Moon

This phase is good for banishing and rejecting emotions, situations and people that affect you negatively. In other words, get rid of whatever is no longer serving you.

– Dark Moon

This is the period of 3 days prior to the New Moon. Traditionally, no magic is performed at this time, but this is a good time for meditation and contemplation.

Chapter 5 Wicca Magic

The Secret of Wicca Magic

Magic is the art of causing change in consciousness, in accordance with our Will.

Just like there are the *placebo* and *nocebo* effects, there are also many cases where you do a spell for someone to get a job, and they get a job. But, is this always ethical? If someone else who was shortlisted for the interview was a single mother who needed money more than you did, was it right for you to use the magic to get the job?

There are also cases where you carry a talisman to get pregnant, but apart from that, you do very little about getting pregnant, and a colleague at work gets pregnant instead. Or you wear a talisman to win a lotto ticket, but often forget to buy the lotto ticket and are furious when you find out that your brother won the lotto (even though he didn't carry a talisman or had a spell cast for this purpose).

What this means, is that magic, ie spells or talismans, can "leak" into someone else's life.

For your dream to come true you have to be actively involved in making it happen. Just casting a spell, or creating a talisman, and then forgetting all about it while expecting to get what you want, is not how magic works. Just like you won't get a job unless you keep on applying for a job, and you won't find new love if you stay at home waiting to be discovered, you have to help the magic work for you.

Another thing to bear in mind when it comes to spells, is that you shouldn't expect to always to get exactly what you wanted. When what you get is not exactly what you hoped for, remember that it's better than nothing.

So, how does Wicca magic actually works? Just like most things that cannot be proved scientifically, this is not easy to explain. It probably has something to do with the Earth's electromagnetic field.

We know that all animals, and some people, are sensitive to electromagnetic fields. These fields affect us in many ways, although most of us have lost the ability to pick-up and recognize these vibrations.

It's believed that magical energy is somehow transmitted via the Earth's magnetic field. Although science has so far failed to explain how magic works (it claims it doesn't), scientific studies do show that meditation, visualization, and prayer affect our subconscious mind and indirectly transform our psyche. Perhaps magic works in a similar way.

The energy that powers magic, ie that transforms your intent into reality, is very real and happens all the time. That energy is your intent. For your intent to manifest into a tangible result, you have to boost it with fire (ie you have to feel real passion about what you are trying to achieve with your spell). But how the Universe transforms your intent into reality, is something no one has been able to explain so far. Suffice it to say that your passion, ie the pain, rage, love or hope you project when you cast a spell, is all the Universe needs to grant your wish.

White, Black or Grey Magic

According to Wiccan Rede, you can do any kind of magic, as long as it does no harm. What's "harmful" is relative, and depends on one's cultural, geographical and social background. However, the bottom line is magic in itself cannot be good or bad, it is your intention that makes it such. Magic is simply a tool, and the way you use it will make it white, black or grey.

So, although there is no clear distinction between types of magic, these are some of the main differences between white, black and grey magic:

? White magic

This is the type of magic you do to help someone or to gain enlightenment. It is usually done with the permission of the person you are doing this for. The kind of spells which fall into this category are love, friendship, blessing, protection, fertility, growing, dream, and healing spells.

? Black magic

You usually do black magic when you want to harm or manipulate someone else, and it's usually done without the permission of the person involved in this magic. If successful, such spells can have a disastrous effect the on the other person's life and are therefore considered potentially dangerous. Also, whether a spell is black or white is a relatve thing. When you do a love spell, so that a certain person falls in love with you, but that person is married with children, which means their marriage will be dissolved and the children will lose one parent, just so that you can have what you want, then what is white magic to you, becomes black magic for the spouse whose partner you are about to steal. The following spells fall into black magic category: death, hurt, resurrection, revenge, bad luck or nightmare spells.

? Grey magic

Everything that is neither black nor white, falls into this category. Grey magic is believed to be an intention to help someone, without asking that person for permission to do that kind of magic on their behalf.

With spells, the most important thing is your intention, ie your motivation (to help or to harm) and this is what makes magic black or white. If you cast a spell to help someone get a job, without them knowing you are doing this, this is grey magic. It's also important for people involved in spell casting spells to understand what they are getting themselves into, ie be conscious of the consequences a spell can trigger, not just for the person the spell was cast for, but for their families.

The Power of Magic: Healing, Revenge, Curses

There is a lot of debate going on about when you are morally justified to do black magic. For example, if someone is harassing you, or preventing you from getting what you want, or undermining your self-confidence, is it OK to use black magic to stop them from continuing to harm you?

How far would you be prepared to go to get what you want, or to prevent someone from stopping you get what you want?

Revenge, Curses, Hex

5 things to consider before doing Black Magic:

– Consider white magic whenever you can

Are you interested in black magic just for personal gain, or to help others? What is so bad that you have to use black magic to deal with it? If you want to help someone who is struggling with an abusive relationship, rather than do a spell to destroy the abuser, perhaps doing a white magic spell to help the abused gain self-confidence would be a better approach. How far would you go to stop such abuse.

– Understand the basics of a black magic ritual

There are many ways of performing such a ritual, and just like other spells, it starts with casting a Circle and using candles, herbs, crystals or charms to draw out the spirits. You will also need to know which mantra to use for each spell. If you are planning to place a curse or hex on someone, always consider the consequences. According to Wiccan Rede whatever you put forth, comes back to you threefold. Make sure the outcome of what you hope to get is worth the risk you are taking.

– Performing a black magic spell

Cast a Circle and draw the symbol of a pentagram in the air inside the circle (with a stick or a wand). Choose a quiet place, outdoors if possible, but remember that spirits are known to stay away from crowded, noisy places. Step inside the Circle, focus on your intent. You will need a lot of energy to complete the spell. You must not be distracted. Say the mantra (each spell needs a different one). If you are summoning demons (or deities), you must know the names of those you want to invoke. When you're done, give thanks and close the Circle. Wait for the results, as well as for the evil you may have caused. Treat the devil spirits with respect. They sometimes hurt even those who invoke them.

– To place a hex

Make a poppet from black cloth and fill it with earth, a few small crystals and hair and nail clippings from the person you want to hex. Sew up the head to close the poppet. Draw a sacred circle and draw a pentagram inside it. Light black candles around the circle before you step inside. Stand inside and speak the words of your spell over the poppet. Repeat them three times. Traditional hex mantra goes something like this:

"I bind your feet from bringing you to harm me. I bind your hands from reaching out to harm me. I bind your mouth from spreading tales to harm me. I bind your mind from sending energy to harm me."

Let the candles burn down. Give thanks and close the Circle.

Healing

Our physical health is affected by our thoughts and emotions, so true healing needs to take place on all levels of our being - physical, emotional and spiritual. Healing spells can help you bring yourself into harmony with the natural healing energies, and correct the imbalances that stress, unhealthy living habits or negative mindset have created.

The three most common types of healing:

1. Spiritual healing

This is also called the "mind body connection" type of healing. Unfortunately, spiritual healing does not work for everyone. Ancient cultures have known about this for a long time, but Western medicine has only recently recognized that just like there is the *placebo* effect (the power to heal oneself if positive thinking prevails), there is also the *nocebo* effect (the power not to heal, if negative thinking prevails.

Simply put, this means that the power to heal, or not to heal, lies with us, and it usually depends on how much we really want to live. Many people die even after going through complex and expensive treatments, simply because they are tired of life or because they believe they are beyond help. In either case, there is very little anyone can do for them.

Spiritual healing can help people in many different ways. It may completely cure someone but can also encourage them to be more positive about life in general, and about their own health in particular. This is in line with the holistic medicine philosophy, which claims that we are all responsible for our own health.

Those who give spiritual healing, develop spiritually faster than others. And the more spiritually they develop, the better healers the become.

2. Contact healing

This kind of healing is often called "touch" healing, because it involves placing of hands, yours or somebody else's on the place which needs to be healed (including the soul).

Healing spells can be used as a substitute for contact healing.

3. Absent healing

Absent healing is about sending healing energy to someone who is physically distant from you, and usually involves visualization, mantras, prayers, chanting, etc. The key thing during absence healing session is to visualize the person you are healing as healthy and strong.

4. Self-healing

We can all self-heal. That's how we, as a species, survived for millions of years, and that's how many indigenous people still fight disease, trauma, injury. Self-healing is based on energy, so raising your energy, eg by rubbing your hands together and placing them on the part of the body that requires healing, or even just imagining this energy from your hands going to the affected part of the body (physical or emotional), you are healing yourself.

Black Magic Spells

These are a few example of Black Magic spells, but before casting them, make sure you can live with the consequences that these spells could trigger not just for the person they are aimed at, but for their families and even for you.

Bad luck spell

You will need: 1 small black candle, a piece of paper

Dim the lights in the room where the spell will be cast. Cast a Circle or sit in front of your altar. Light the candle. Invoke the deities you want to work with. Write the name of the person you want to cause bad luck for on the piece of paper and repeat:

Great God and Goddess (name them), make him/her to (name the person and state what you want to happen to them). This is my will, so mote it be.

Burn the paper on the candle, and wait for the candle to burn down. Give thanks and close the Circle.

Guilt spell

You will need: 1 small black candle, piece of paper

Write the person's name on the paper and next to their name write what you think the person is guilty of (eg murder, violence, theft, harassment, cheating, etc). Visualize this person doing the crimes you are accusing them of. Light the candle and burn the paper focusing on this person. This spell will not make the person die, but will make them feel guilty all the time. Wait until the candle burns down, give thanks and close the Circle.

Nightmare hex

You will need: 1 small black candle, picture of the person you want to hex (if you don't have a picture, then some of their personal belongings, however, you need to know what they look like).

Find out which deities are associated with night, darkness and dreams. There are many, so invoke the one you feel most comfortable with, eg Greek God Hypnos, Roman Goddess Luna, Slavic Goddess Zorya, etc. Light the candle and repeat these words three times while looking at the person picture and visualize them having horrible nightmares:

God/Goddess of dreams (name the deity), make (name of the person) dream of horrible things for ten nights. Make him/her have nightmares every night for ten nights. Make their sleep something they will dread for ten nights. After ten nights, make (name of the person) well again So mote it be.

Burn the picture on the candle and leave some offering for the God/ Goddess (you can leave some food out for the birds or stray animals). Wait for the candle to burn down, give thanks and close the Circle.

Fear spell

You will need: strong negative emotion, such as hatred, rage, jealousy, envy.

Fill the air around you with dark and/or chaotic energy. Sit in a messy, dirty room, and fill the air with your malice, hatred and anger. To do this, you need to focus on your own negative emotions. What is it that's making you so angry, envious, or hateful? Say it out loud and then focus on this emotion. Stay with it until you start boiling with rage. You now have sufficient negative energy inside you to transfer it to the other person. Start chanting:

Hatred and malice and anger I feel. My insane side has been fuelled by you. Vengeance is just And you are worthy of my punishment. Feel the force of my lost pain, Feel the force of my lost anguish. Let terror haunt you, Strip all defences from you, As long as there is darkness in my heart.

Say this three time, your voice must show your contempt, hatred, envy. Send all the hateful energy you have summoned towards this person, and visualize a wall of black smoke forming around them, preventing them from getting out. Lock him inside.

Remember that some spells are sent back to the person who cast them, so be careful. If the person has protected himself energetically from psychic attacks, your spell is in vain. This is a powerful ,but emotionally very draining spell. Before casting it make sure you have enough energy to go through with it. People are known to pass out while casting spells like this.

White Magic Spells

Blessing spell

You will need: 1 big white candle, essential oil mix, something to represent who/what you are blessing (photograph, personal item, symbol, etc).

Carve the person or the image of what you are trying to bless on the candle, then dress it with essential oil mix. To further empower the spell, place the photograph of the person or the thing you want to bless (eg a house, a boat) under the candle, or if it's a personal item, place it next to the candle.

For seven days, burn the candle for ten minutes a day, at roughly the same time. At the start of the ritual each day, redress the candle with essential oil mix and repeat these words:

[Name], may you be blessed May all good things come to you May nothing whatsoever harm you May your heart be light May your travels be safe May your health be good May your mind be sound May your friendships sustain you May you be blessed in every way.

You can change the text and add what you wish for this person (eg to get a job, to get a child, to recover from illness, etc).

Healing spells

The reason spells DO work is that while preparing them, and while performing them, you force yourself to focus on the issue you are addressing, and sometimes, all it takes for someone to heal, or find a solution to a problem, or feel calmer, is to focus on the issue and channel their personal energy in the right direction.

Try to make the space where you will cast the spell clean, bright, and filled with fresh air.

Candle Healing Spell

You will need: 2 white candles, 1 green candle, a bowl, water, salt

Cast the Circle or sit in front of your altar. Place the bowl in the middle (of the Circle or the altar, whichever you're using). Place the white candles on each side of the bowl and the green one in front of it.Light the candles. Focus on the candles and visualize a green healing light coming out of them. Focus on this light and channel it either to yourself or to the person you want to heal. Repeat these words three times:

"Oh great goddess of the moon
  Please heal this body you gave birth to
  Let this energy flow into the wound
  And heal it right
  No scar nor pain in sight.
  This is my will so mote it be"
  Wait for all three candles to burn down, give thanks and close the Circle.

Disease Banishing Spell

You will need: red or black cord, black candle, open fire, 1 big piece of clear quartz crystal

Cast a Circle or sit in front of the altar. Place the crystal in the middle (of the Circle or the Altar) and the candle next to it. Light the candle. Bind the part of the body that requires healing (eg head, arm, leg, stomach) with the red or black cord. Focus on the affected part of the body. Say:

I bind the disease residing in (name the part of the body). May it leave my body forever. Great Goddess (name the deity you are invoking), please take the disease away. The disease is bound into the cord and flames will destroy it. So mote it be!

Untie the cord and throw it immediately into the fire. Focus on your intent. Visualize the disease being destroyed with the flames. Focus on the burning cord until it had been devoured by the fire. Close your eyes and while you wait for the candle to burn down, visualize yourself free of pain forever.

Give thanks and close the Circle.

Chapter 6 Creating Magic

Setting Up Altar

Altar is a focal point for Wiccans, a sacred space where they meditate, visualize, cast spells, perform rituals, and commune with their deities.

If you are starting on a Wiccan path, the first thing you should do, is create an altar, which will serve as a starting point for everything else you do in Wicca.

Your altar should always be clean and vibrant, for dust and clutter prevent energy from flowing smoothly. Decorate it with beautiful, meaningful things which symbolize the four elements, and not just with souvenirs you bring from holidays. Your altar is a sacred space even when you are not using it in a ritual. If possible keep it protected from prying eyes, and don't let others touch the items displayed there.

If you can, set aside a small table for your altar, but this is often not possible. No matter how small your altar is, make sure you have sufficient space to move around it, or to reach the items placed there.

You can keep items on a permanent display, or you can change the "set up" for each ritual. Whatever you do, remember that your altar should "speak to you" and that the items placed there should resonate with you and represent your own values and beliefs. Therefore, rather than buy expensive tools, use what you have or create items that are meaningful to YOU.

Things to consider when creating an altar:
? Do you want an indoor or outdoor altar
Traditionally, Pagans worship under the sky and Nature is there temple. However, things have changed and most of us live in crowded, and crime-ridden cities where privacy necessary for a ritual is becoming hard to find. Besides, many rituals are performed under the Full Moon, so doing this outdoors, may not be safe unless you have a garden). There is also the issue of weather. Having an indoor altar is much more practical because you can concentrate on the ritual without having to worry about privacy, safety, or rain. Inside your home, choose a place where you are least likely to be disturbed,

and where visitors are unlikely to see or hold your altar items (this is usually a bedroom).

? Consider the location

Your altar can face any direction, and it's usually the East, where the Sun rises, however, many Pagan spells call for the spell caster to face the North. Depending on the size of your altar and the location where you plan to put it, this may or may not be easy. If, due to lack of space, you are forced to have your altar facing West, this is not a major problem and should not affect the efficiency of the spell. However, whenever possible try to face the quarter you need most help from (eg North for finance, South for passion, etc). Altars are often placed on dresser tables, inside drawers, on bookshelves, windowsills, or even chairs. Some people even have an altar box, so they carry their altar with them, and can do a ritual even when away from home.

? Consider the style and size

As mentioned earlier, Wicca is a reconstructed religion of pre-Christian Europe, so most of the deities and rituals are based on those cultures. However, you may choose to follow beliefs of ancient of current Pagan religions from outside Europe, such as Hinduism, Taoism, animism, etc. That is fine, but try not to mix-and-match too many different items on your altar (or in your rituals). If you go with Hindu deities and practices, stick to those, don't mix them with Celtic or Nordic ones. Your altar is a very personal thing and should reflect your spirituality and values.

Decorating your altar:

– Decide on items

Figure out what symbols you want on your altar, especially if it's a small one. What will you represent the five elements with? What about the Goddess and the God?

– Decide on deities

Which Goddess and God will be dominant in your magic? Do you have their images, statues or are you going to represent them symbolically with an item (eg the Hindu Goddess Lakshmi is often represented with a bunch of fresh flowers). Some deities are symbolized with particular colour, so you can use candles of that colour as a symbol of that deity. Some deities have their totem animals (eg cat, owl, hare) so you can use their images or statues to represent the goddess.

– Mark the four quarters and the Centre

Decide what will go in the centre of the altar. This are usually your matron/patron deities, or an object, eg candle of the colour which represents the element of Spirit, eg purple or white. You can also use a big crystal. Use something significant, something that stands out. Symbolic items representing other elements should be placed on the side, in the part of the altar corresponding to that particular elements, eg Earth in the North, Fire in the South, etc.

– Have stuff in store to use on special occasions

It's best not to have the altar cluttered, however, you will occasionally need special items for specific spells eg love, job, healing, etc so keep items that you can use for these occasional spells somewhere safe, but don't keep all you have displayed on your altar all the time. For example, you can occasionally use jewelry or coins (to boost your wealth spells), flowers and herbs (to help with the healing or love spells), etc.

– Sacred cloth

The altar should always be covered with a cloth used only for that purpose. Choose the colour that you feel most drawn to, or choose it according to the element you need most help from (eg brown for earth, blue for water, etc).

Spells

Once you have set up your altar, it's time to put it to use, ie to start casting spells.

Crystals in Ritual

Coming from the centre of the earth, crystals represent the Earth element whose main function is to offer stability, security, and help with all sorts of practical issues (eg money, family, job, property, etc).

Which crystals you will use will depend on what you hope your spell to help you with. For love you will need stones whose colour can fire-up passion (eg red and orange), for healing you'll need colours that are calming and soothing (eg blue or white), for friendship and love spells you'll use pink and white crystals, for financial matters green or brown work best, etc.

Ritual to banish anxiety
Crystals that work best for anxiety are citrine (for its cleansing properties), amethyst (for its protective properties) and hematite (it will help you ground).
Keep your space (ie your home or your room) clean and tidy. Regularly open the windows to let fresh air in. Place the crystals (citrine, amethyst and hematite) in a prominent place in the room you use most. Put some salt in the corners of all your rooms, or in the room you spend most time in. When you feel yourself sinking into a state of anxiety, get up, clap your hands, stamp your feet or sing. Use lavender or chamomile incense sticks to clear the energy in your living space
Distance healing spell

You will need: 3 white candles, a piece clear quartz crystal, peppermint incense, a picture of the person you want to heal.

Decide which Goddess you are going to invoke for this healing spell. Cast a Circle or sit in front of your altar. Place the picture in the centre of the Circle (or altar) and the crystal on top of it. Place the candles around it. Place the incense in front of you. Light the candles.

Invoke the Goddess and ask her to empower your spell. Look at the picture and focus on your intent. Raise your energy in the way that suits you most, eg dancing, singing, drumming or visualizing. When you feel you have raised enough energy, direct it toward the crystal. Visualize a protective ring of white light forming around that person, shielding them from disease, pain and suffering.

When you are done, and when the candle had burned down, give thanks and close the Circle. Sit quietly for a few moments to ground yourself. Have a glass of water.

Crystal talisman to help with self-acceptance

Agate crystal pendants or small piece of this crystal carried with you can help you open up and communicate better. Agate will also encourage you to accept yourself. It serves as a powerful protection from negative energies, eg toxic people or environments.

Attract Abundance talisman

A big piece of green calcite, placed in a prominent place at home, where you will often see it, will help boost your career, prosperity as well as fertility. It is a powerful wealth-attracting stone. Look at it and touch it often.

Herbal Magic

Herbs have magic of their own and people have been tapping into their healing, calming, energizing or mood-enhancing properties since prehistoric times. Wicca herbal magic is the art of getting the plants to work for you by empowering your ritual, healing your body and mind, or clearing your living space of negative energy.

Each plant has a vibrational energy, which, combined with a focused intent, creates powerful magic.

Headache relief spell

You will need: a glass of Full Moon water, 1 lavender scented candle, 1 teaspoon lavender flowers, 1 piece clear quartz crystal.

Pour boiling water over the dry lavender flowers. Cast a Circle or sit in front of your altar. Light the candle, close your eyes and relax. Inhale the lavender steam from the tea cup and say:

"Flowers of purple, heal my head
I will not take to my bed
The pain will flee
O' rising stream take the pain with thee."

Sip the herbal infusion and feel yourself relaxing, and your headache going away. After you have drunk most of the tea, place the crystal in the remaining tea and say:

"Crystal Bright, Bring your shining Light
Take this pain to keep me sane
Right now I feel no mirth
Your power is from the Earth
Send this pain away and make my day!"

Remove the crystal from the cup and place it on your "third eye" (the area right between your eyebrows), lie down for ten minutes and let the crystal absorb the pain. When you are ready (ie when the headache had gone and when the candle had burned down), give thanks, and close the circle. Wash the crystal under running water and put it away.

Warding off depression spell

You will need: Your favourite dry herbs or incense, 1 medium-sized yellow candle.

Perform this ritual in a room/space where your altar can be undisturbed for three days. Cast a Circle or arrange your magic tools on your altar. Focus on your intent, imagining how good it must feel to be happy. Dispel all negative thoughts.

Light the incense or pour boiling water over the herbs, and breathe in the aroma. Invoke the Goddess you want to work with. Imagine a bright yellow light surrounding you and your altar (or Circle if you are sitting inside it).

Hold the candle between your hands and direct all your positive energy to the candle. Light the candle saying:

This candle represents the love and energy I have for myself. As I light this candle, the veil of darkness that is ever present in my mind is lifting. The darkness ceases to exist as the light of this flame glows. Long has the darkness filled my mind, my desire to be happy is intense like the heat of fire. As this candle burns, my spirits are lifting and the negative energy is washing away. I will be happy, my life will be peaceful. I can see myself as I wish to be-happy and free!

Watch the candle burn, and visualize your depression disappear in with the smoke of the candle. Imagine yourself happy, laughing, surrounded by friends and family.

When you're ready, give thanks and close the Circle. Repeat this for two more nights. On the last night, after the candle has burned down, collect the leftover wax and bury it in the garden. You are free of depression.

Herbal Ritual for the Dead

When casting a Circle for the Samhain Sabbat, you can set the boundaries by marking them with flower petals and herbs such as rose, rosemary, juniper, bay, parsley, yew and whatever other fresh flowers or herbs you can find on 31 October (this will largely depend on where you live).

Dim the lights. Cast a Circle and define the boundaries with herbs. Step inside. Mark the four quarters, invoke the elements and invoke the deities you want to work with for this spell. Light the candle. If you have a picture of the deceased, place it under the candle. If you have some of their personal possessions, place them next to the candle.

Focus on who you want to communicate with. Visualize this person, try to hear (ie remember the sound of their voice, smell the perfume or aftershave they used, feel them near you). Ask them to join you. Repeat these words while sprinkling the Circle (or the altar if you are using it instead of the Circle) with the flower petals, leaves and springs:

The wheel of life turns,
The cycle of rebirth continues.
Those beyond life,
You are remembered today.

Repeat this several times, but if nothing happens, ie if the deceased does not appear, don't push it.

Focus on what you want to achieve, ie who you are hoping to meet. Inhale the scent of fresh herbs, be as relaxed as you can.

If the deceased appears ask them a question and wait for the answer. If you hear nothing, go to the next question. Do not ask more than three questions. When you are done, give thanks and close the Circle. Communing with the dead can be stressful and exhausting, so sit quietly for a few moments, and have a glass of water to ground yourself.

Candle Spellwork

Candles represent the element of Fire, and are used in all spells simply because they provide additional energy. Adding fire to some aspects of your life (love, career, health, etc) simply means boosting your energy in that department. However, remember that the most powerful part of the candle is not the size, colour or shape - it is the flame. The flame, ie the fire element we are invoking everytime we light a candle, is what creates magic, boosts passion or destroys.

Worry banishing spell

You will need: 1 black candle, 1 piece of paper

Cast your Circle or sit in front of the altar (where you have set up the tools for the ritual). Draw a pentacle on the paper and place in inside the Circle or on the altar. Invoke your matron and patron deities. Light the candle and start chanting:

"(name your deities) I call on you to banish what is causing me harm. With this candle, please burn the harm away".

Visualize the cause of your anxiety, and as the candle burns, and wax melts, imagine your worries disappearing. Wait for the candle to burn down, give thanks and close the Circle.

Love spell to help you find a soulmate

You will need: 4 small red candles, 2 small white candles

Cast a Circle, or sit in front of your altar. Place the red candles all around you, to mark each of the quarters (north, south, east, west). If your space and the position of the altar allow, face the North. Close your eyes, breathe slowly, relax. Focus on your desire. Open your eyes. Invoke the Goddess. Invoke the element of Earth and light the red candle placed in the North. Turn around towards the South and invoke the element of Fire. Repeat will all four elements. Then sit back in your original position and light the white candles. Place one on your left and the other one on your right. Say:

As I will it, I bring into my life the soulmate that I crave, the love that I deserve. I am a powerful creator, and as I will, shall be.

Hold the white candles in your hands and tilt the tops till the flames become one.

Say: As we come together as one, I bring my wish to pass. So mote it be!

Visualize your soulmate and stay with this image for a while. See yourself happy and in love. See yourself walking, laughing, and travelling with your partner. Visualize what he looks like, how tall he is, what colour hair he has, what his hobbies are, etc. Then, blow out the combined flame of the white candles, saying:

I release this intent into the universe.

Face each of the red candles and ask the element they represent to empower your intent. Blow out the candle. Repeat this will all four red candles.

Give thanks and close the Circle.

Chapter 7 Life, Death & Rebirth

Life Cycles

Wiccans not only honour the cycles of nature through celebrating Sabbats, they also mark and honor their own cycles of life.

From the pure biological point of view, a life cycle represents a series of changes that an organism undergoes as it develops, grows, matures and dies.

The most common rites of passage for Wiccans:

– Birth

During the ceremony, the Goddess is asked to bless the newborn arrival.

– Marriage (handfasting)

With this ceremony, Wiccans celebrate vows that a couple will stay together for eternity

– Growing up

Just like many indigenous cultures, Wiccans celebrate transition from childhood to puberty, adolescence and adulthood

– Growing old

Wiccans value the wisdom of old age, and they honour aging by "croning" ceremonies (for women) and "elderhood" ceremonies for men.

– Death

For Wiccans death is not the end of existence, but simply a process of transformation. They remember their dead and speak with them on the Day of the Dead (Samhain).

The Samhain, the Day of the Dead, which takes place on 31 October is the most important Wiccan festival. Not only does it mark the beginning of a Wiccan New Year, but it is also a time when the boundaries between the worlds of the dead and the living become thin, and it becomes easy to contact the dead.

On the physical level, at the end of October, we watch the earth transform itself and slowly die for the season. Traditionally, Wiccans use this time to remember the dead and contemplate the endless cycle of life, death and rebirth, both in nature, and in their own lives.

Rituals performed on Samhain should reflect that transition and altars should be decorated with symbols of life and death, eg a white and a black candle, a red and a white ribbon, sprigs of fresh rosemary or other herb, dead leaves, etc.

When celebrating Samhain, if at all possible, cast the Circle outside and light a fire. Invoke your deities. Mark the four quarter of the Circle.

The traditional Samhain ritual:

Place the rosemary (or whatever herb you are using) on the altar (or inside the Circle) and say:

Samhain is here, and it is a time of transitions.
   The winter approaches, and the summer dies.
   This is the time of the Dark Mother[1],
   a time of death and of dying.
   This is the night of our ancestors[2]
   and of the Ancient Ones.

Light the black candle saying:
   "*The Wheel of the Year turns once more, and we cycle into darkness*".

Light the white candle saying:
   "*At the end of that darkness comes light. And when it arrives, we will celebrate once more*".

Take the ribbons saying:
   "*White for life, black for death, red for rebirth. I bind these strands together remembering those we have lost*".

As you braid the three ribbons together, remember your dead. Start chanting:
   As the corn will come from grain,
   All that dies will rise again.
   As the seeds grow from the earth,
   We celebrate life, death and rebirth.

After the ceremony, close the Circle, thank the deities who have witnessed your ritual, and take the braided ribbons to keep on your altar.

---

1.   https://www.thoughtco.com/mabon-ritual-to-honor-the-dark-mother-2562295

2.   https://www.thoughtco.com/ancestor-worship-in-pagan-cultures-2562898

Reincarnation

Reincarnation is the philosophical concept that a living being can start a new life in a different physical body after its biological death. This process is also referred to as rebirth, and was part of many religious beliefs, eg Spiritism, Theosophy, Eckankar.

Many of the major religions believe in reincarnation, eg Hinduism, Jainism, Buddhism, Sikhism. Their belief systems are based on the idea that when the body disintegrates at death, the mind continues to exist and simply moves on to the next life.

According to this philosophy it's wrong to try and end suffering (physical or emotional) by committing suicide. For if we accept that the mind lives on after death, it simply means that death will not be the end to suffering and that it will simply take on another form. People should address the cause of suffering, not run away from it.

So, what happens when we die?

For obvious reasons it's difficult to know for sure, but according to the spiritual beliefs of religions who believe in reincarnation, as our mind becomes quiet and slowly dies down (death does not happen instantaneously, even when the heart stops working), we enter a kind of deep sleep. After a while we enter into a dream-like state that is typical of a time between death and rebirth. After a few days of weeks, the intermediate state ends and we take rebirth. We are born as a different person, without ever remembering our previous life.

Proof of Reincarnation

In cultures where reincarnation is part of the formal religion, it is believed that by observing present mental tendencies and predispositions of individuals, it's easy to guess what they must have been in their previous lives.

It's surprisingly easy to spot typical character traits of very young children, and predict what their character is going to be like. While some are good natured and kind, others show early signs of cruelty, selfishness, aggression, envy or tendency towards bullying.

The fact that children, even twins, sometimes exhibit extreme differences, even though they come from the same parents, is believed to be the sign of what they were in previous lives.

Those who believe in reincarnation claim that mental tendencies are developed through repeated actions over a long period of time. So, if a child of 4, exhibits clear signs of bullying, it is obvious that it must have developed those traits in its previous life, for it is too young to have had time to develop them in this life. In other words, a child's current values and behaviours are a sign of who and what they could have been in the previous life.

What effect do our past lives have on us?

When someone feels passionately for or against something, it's believed to be a sign of what they had experience with in their past life. For example, if someone learns a particular foreign language easily and speaks it fluently, it could mean that that was their mother tongue in the previous life. Or, someone who is deeply religious or spiritual, probably lived that way in his previous life as well.

The Afterlife

Most of us have, at some point asked the question, "what happens when we die".

From the biological point of view, science knows exactly what happens to flesh and bones, how fast and when. But, when it comes to human consciousness, no one knows for sure.

In 2010, one of the most respected scientist in the world, an expert in regenerative medicine, Robert Lanza, created a theory that our consciousness does not die with us, but moves on.

According to Lanza, if the body generates consciousness, then consciousness dies when the body dies. But, new studies suggest that if the body receives consciousness in the same way that a TV set receives satellite signals, that means that consciousness does not end at the death of the physical vehicle (eg when a TV set breaks down, it doesn't mean the satellite signals have stopped, but that the TV is simply unable to receive them, although they are still being transmitted, and maybe picked up by another set).

There are many documented cases of individuals who were clinically dead (showing no brain activity), who remember everything that was happening to them on the medical table at the time when they were clinically dead.

There are many instances where "dead" individuals later described in detail the conversation that the staff were having while he was lying "dead".

Unfortunately, modern science operates on the premise that unless something cannot be proven in a lab, it is automatically discredited.

If this is true it means that what ancient philosophies, such as Ayurveda have been claiming for thousands of years, we are only beginning to slowly discover in the 21st century.

The concept of afterlife is the belief that an individual's consciousness continues to exist after the death of the physical body. This concept is treated in many different ways by different religions but it usually takes place in a spiritual realm, and according to this belief, the rebirths continue until the individual is granted entry into a spiritual realm.

All religions based on Abrahamic tradition, claim that the dead go to a place (either a heaven or a hell) from which they cannot return. Where they will go is decided by the God. On the other hand, religions which believe in reincarnation, believe that how many times a person will be reborn depends on their actions, rather than by somebody else's decision.

Contacting the Dead

There are many reasons why someone would want to contact their dead. Ancestor worship is a major part of many indigenous religions. For Wiccans, it is traditionally done during the festival of Samhain, at night, around a fire.

When casting a Circle for this ritual, it is necessary to create a protection circle around the area you are going to be working in. Proceed with welcoming the spirits you want to work with in your ritual. This ceremony is best learnt from experience, so if you are new to Wicca or if you've never tried to contact the dead, it's best you perform this with the help of someone who had done this before.

Most religions, both formal and indigenous, feel that spirits of the dead should be allowed to leave this world as soon as possible. Although some people maintain contact with the dead who serve as their guides and mentors, spirits of the dead are often malevolent and can cling to a person causing harm. Besides, most people feel reluctant to deal with the dead, and it's true that communing with the deceased can be extremely painful, disturbing and exhausting, so before you do it, make sure it's worth the effort.

Wiccans feel free to contact the dead during Samhain festival, but even then they never hold seances or invite spirits who are not keen to join in the conversation. At Samhain, you can try to contact your loved ones who had passed away, but only if they agree to show up. Wiccans never coerce or force such an encounter.

People who wish to communicate with the other world, usually have things to say to someone who had passed away, that they didn't have a chance to say while they were alive.

There are many ways to contact the dead, but it is usually done at the altar, which for that occasion is decorated with photographs and items that remind you of that person, or by arranging dinner for the dead.

Traditionally, dinner for the dead is served in black plates, on black tablecloth, and with black napkins. If you are using the candles, they should also be black. There should be no other light in the room. This dinner is called The Silent Dinner. No one at the table should speak throughout the dinner.

The Silent Dinner procedure:

- Prepare the place where the Silent Dinner will take place by cleansing it with incense. Reserve the place at the head of the table for the Spirits. When everyone is seated, join the hands and bless the food. After dinner, leave the room after you've silently said goodbye to all the Spirits you have invoked to participate in the dinner.

How best to communicate with the dead?

– Speak directly to them

Focus on the dead person, try to "feel" their presence in the room. Speak directly to them through the power of your mind. Focus on the image of the deceased. Ask a question and wait until you receive a reply.

– Ask for "yes" or "no" answer to simple questions

This kind of conversation is usually achieved by asking the spirits to give one knock for yes, and two for no.

This is one of the most complex Wicca rituals, so it's best not to attempt it until you've been practicing Wicca for some time. If you are angry with the deceased, don't ask them to join you so that you could use the opportunity to tell them what you think of them.

If, on the other hand, you feel afraid, upset or anxious about meeting them, leave it for some other time, because your negative energy could prevent them from showing up. Do this ritual only when you feel calm, relaxed and happy to see your loved ones again. Although the experience can leave you exhausted, this should be a joyful and not stressful event.

Chapter 8 Practical Wicca

Becoming Wiccan

A Wiccan is often described as a witch, so what does it mean to be a witch? The literal translation of the word witch is "wise" , because in ancient times witches were respected for their knowledge of healing herbs, as well as for their ability to perform magic that could heal or harm people. Therefore, witchcraft is "the craft of the wise".

However, becoming a Wiccan does not automatically make you a witch. There are different levels of involvement with this religion, as well as many different paths and traditions to choose from. However, a true witch is someone who:

- Is a healer

- Loves nature, and

- Honours the Goddess

Depending on the tradition you choose to follow, there may be an initiation ritual that you have to go through. Some traditions insist on this, others don't. Then, you can choose to belong to a coven or decide to be a solitary witch.

Being a solitary witch may be a lot simpler and sometimes more effective, however, if you enjoy group work, if you don't like the idea of having to learn about Wicca from books, or if you take pleasure in participating in sophisticated rituals, perhaps it's best to join a coven.

However, if you decide to be a solitary witch, how do you start? Fortunately, you can find a lot of information on witchcraft on Internet.

Steps to becoming a solitary witch:

– Read as much on Wicca as you can

– Join Wicca Forums

– Choose a path or tradition that most appeals to you

– Start small and gradually increase your involvement (eg start by collecting items for your altar, learn how to cast a circle, etc)

– Choose one or two Sabbats to celebrate (you can do all of them if you like)

– Choose an Esbat you want to celebrate every month (it's usually the New or the Full Moon). Sabbat and Esbats celebrations can be a complex or a simple affair, and how you choose to do them will depend on how much time, and resources you have

– Start meditating

– Learn about visualization, for this is very important for spell casting

– Find your Wiccan Goddess and God

Religion is a very personal thing and there is no one way of practicing it, regardless of which religion it is. When it comes to Wicca, members are encouraged to use their intuition and imagination as much as they can, so whatever instructions you find, remember that they are merely guidelines, and that the type and level of your involvement, is entirely up to you.

Aligning Yourself with the World of Spirit

Spell casting and magic is very much part of being a Wiccan, but doing magic is much more than performing rituals someone else has written, where you sometimes not even understand why you are doing, or saying, certain things.

Real magic comes from deep within, but for this you have to be aligned to the world of spirit. How do you do that? This comes easier to some than to others, for we are not all equally spiritually inclined, nor equally able to pick up vibes from our environment.

How do you become more spiritual? Many believe that spirituality is not something you can learn from a book or a course, and that you have to be born that way, however, there are ways of refining your mind and soul to be more in line with the sacred.

We live in a competitive, aggressive, and increasingly stressful world, where to survive people have to become tough, materialistically-oriented, and goal-focused, which doesn't help one's spiritual development.

However, we are not just a physical body. We are also spiritual, mental, and emotional beings, and to align yourself with the spiritual realm, you have to "purify" all levels of your being.

4 ways of spiritual purification:

– To purify your spiritual body you have to live morally, believe in a Higher Power and acknowledge and correct your past mistakes, or at least make sure you never make them again.

– To purify your mental body you should develop a positive attitude, and fill your mind with loving, optimistic thoughts.

– To purify your emotional body you should have only positive emotions, avoid toxic relationships and situations, and get involved in arts, music, or voluntary work.

– To purify your physical body you should adopt healthy living habits, eg healthy diet, sufficient rest, physical exercise, and good personal hygiene.

Sometimes, all you need to do to find your spirit is to slow down and listen. You'll be surprised how much you can hear when you sit in silence. Let go of situations, careers or people that make you feel small or that crush your soul. Instead, seek opportunities, people and places that raise your vibrations. It's not always easy being a spiritual person in the material world, but it's certainly worth a try.

Developing Skills and Knowledge

Wicca is mainly an experiential religion, although a lot can be learned from books, magazines, blogs, forums, lectures, and from other Wiccans. However, magic requires a certain level of psychic development which can be achieved through certain spiritual practices, such as yoga breathing, repeating mantra, saying prayers, and other activities which raise your vibrational rate and enable you to become more receptive to the world of Spirit.

3 simple steps to raise your vibrations:

? Develop your intuitive powers

You can do this through visualization, dream-work or circle-work. Those with good intuition are highly sensitive to feelings and thoughts of others, and easily pick-up vibrational changes in their environment. This can be of enormous help in spell work.

? Meditate regularly

People meditate in most unusual ways. Some do it by sitting for hours in a lotus position, others by gazing into a candle flame or an open fire, some prefer to focus on an object or picture of a deity, still others do it while making bread, walking or gardening. Meditation is about switching off and becoming so relaxed that you become receptive to your subconscious, and how you do it, is up to you.

? Take long, quiet walks in nature

Nature is a great absorber of negativity, and the further away from the noise and pollution you are, the easier it becomes to reconnect with your subconscious.

Although we all possess intuitive powers, most of us have ignored them for so long, they no longer exist. The tricky part is persuading yourself to hear what your inner voice is telling you, because it often isn't what you want to hear. In the noisy, materialistic and distractive world we live in, this is not easy. However, the more you listen to your inner voice, the better at interpreting it you will become.

Ritual: Casting a Circle

According to Aleister Crowley, "magic is the art or science of causing change to occur in conformity with Will".

Rituals are probably the most important aspect of the Wiccan religion. They are performed within the Circle which, once cast, becomes a ritual space.

When you cast a circle, you are symbolically defining the boundaries of a place where you will face your deities, where you may enter the altered state of consciousness, and where magic will happen. This space becomes sacred. The boundaries are "protected" by the symbols of the elements and the deities you decide to invoke before casting a spell.

To cast a Circle you have to open up your energy points, eg chakras, to make yourself the conduit for the energy needed to cast a Circle. You do this by relaxing yourself, and taking 7 slow breaths, visualizing each of your chakras as you do that. Start from the root and finish with the crown chakra.

When you are ready, concentrate your energy in your arm where you are holding the athame (you can use a wand, a branch, or a finger instead) and draw a line in the air around the ritual space.

Mark the cardinal points of the Circle (north, south, east and west) with something that represents an element. Earth is in the north, Air in the east, Fire in the South, and Water in the West. Mark the North with something that represents earth, in the West place something that stands for water, etc.

That way, the space within these elements, which is where you stand, becomes a sacred space where spells can be cast. Whenever possible try to mark the quarters with symbols whose colour match the colour typical of that element (eg brown for Earth, red for Fire, etc).

Traditionally, you should ask for a presence of a Goddess and her consort. These can be deities you have chosen for that particular ritual (eg love spell, healing spell, blessing spell), or you may have your matron and patron deities you work with all the time.

Marking the Circle boundaries with elements:

Air

Place the items representing the element of Air in the East.

If you want to ask Air elementals to help you with your spellwork, invoke sylphs or fairies of trees, flowers and winds.

Ask for the presence of deities you want to work with.

The Water element

Water element belongs to the West.

If you want to ask Water elemental spirits to help you with your spell, invoke nymphs, mermaids or fairies of ponds, lakes and streams.

Ask for the presence of deities you want to work with.

Earth

Earth element belongs to the North quarter of the circle. The primary earth Goddess is Mother Nature or Gaia.

The elemental spirits of earth are tree-spirits, trolls and gnomes Earth colors are brown, black, green and gold so keep this in mind when decorating your altar.

Fire

The fire element is situated in the South of the circle.

It is believed that to connect with fire elementals (salamanders), there has to be a live fire present. However, as this is usually not possible, we have to use a candle instead. Night is the best time to meet with nature spirits of fire, as they are more visible at this time.

Ask for the presence of deities you have chosen to work with.

The Spirit

Spirit is represented in the centre of the Circle. Colours used to represent this element are usually purple or white.

Preparation for spell work

Prepare the space where the spell will be cast by clearing it from clutter and dust. Make sure you will not be disturbed for at least 30 minutes, otherwise there's not much point in casting a Circle. Switch off your phone, take pets out of the room.

To cast a spell, you need to raise your power and the easiest way of doing this is by dancing, clapping your hands, drumming, or using a rattle. Do this for about ten minutes, then shake your arms and legs to ground yourself.

When you have completed your ritual, don't forget to thank the deities and elementals you had invoked to witness your ritual, then close the Circle. As spell casting can be emotionally draining, have a glass of water and sit quietly for a few moments to ground yourself.

Precautions and Mistakes to Avoid for New Wiccans

To avoid traps that many beginners face, and to avoid wasting time, be clear why you want to become a Wiccan.

5 things to bear in mind if you decide to follow a Wiccan path:,

– Understand what Wicca is and isn't about

Before you start practicing magic, know what you're getting yourself into (especially with black magic, be prepared to take the consequences)

– Don't spend a fortune on Wicca tools

Tools are only symbols, and most of what you need for your altar or a spell, you can find in your home, garden or local park (feathers, stones, unusual pieces of wood, etc)

– Don't do spells for others until you've gained sufficienet experience

Practice on yourself for several months. Divination abilities give you power, but don't use it to play with other people's emotions

– Respect others' privacy

Whatever goes on during spell casting, stays with you. Never discuss other people's dreams or problems with anyone.

– If spells don't work

The reason could be that you are not doing them properly, or that they may need to be repeated several times, or that you have chosen the wrong time to ask for something, or that the Universe has a reason not to grant you your wish right now. Be patient, and if nothing happens, try again in couple of weeks.

– Learn about colour therapy

The symbolism of colour is very important in ritual, so learn how you can use colour to boost your spells

– Learn about crystals

Crystals are an essential part of rituals, talismans and altars. Find out as much as you can about their physical, healing, as well as magical properties.

– Learn about herbs

Traditionally, witches are healers, so start by learning healing and magical properties of a few common herbs, and gradually expand your knowledge to include all the herbs available locally. Start collecting or growing your own.

– Learn about energy

Your personal energy is your biggest asset. Protect yourself from those who steal it, by making you feel drained, uncomfortable or "small". Avoid being around such people if you can, if you can't (eg if that's someone you live or work with), spend as little time near them as you can and create a mental barrier so as to prevent your precious energy from being tapped into.

Conclusion

There are many reasons and ways to participate in the magic of Nature-based religions such as Wicca. From developing your intuition, learning visualization, and understanding metaphysical aspects of life, to being closer to Mother Earth and learning to commune with Nature.

Whatever it is you want from a religion, Wicca can provide. But, perhaps the best thing it can do for you is motivate you to slow down and harmonize your life with the seasonal cycles, and come to terms with cycles of your own life, eg the fact that you're getting old and that fewer and fewer opportunities will come your way, or that you are no longer a child and should start taking responsibility for your actions, etc.

Wicca is not only a religious system, it's a way of life and once you start looking at the world around you through Wiccan lense, you'll be surprised how much you'll worldview will change.

Although Wicca is a reconstructed religion of ancient Pagan beliefs, the reason it is so popular in this day and age is because it resonates with the changing mindset of people, eg it is not focused on patriarchal worldview, it is much more tolerant and flexible compared to formal religions, it encourages self-development and personal responsibility.

The growing number of Wicca followers clearly show that a major shift in consciousness is taking place as we speak, and that more and more people realize the importance of balance, both in the environment and in their own lives.

The main advantage of Wicca is that it encourages its followers to slow down, pay attention to the world around them, and allow themselves to be permeated with the healing and nurturing energies of Nature.